One Day with Jesus

One Day with Jesus

Written by
Frank Richardson

Edited by
Franklin Richardson, Jr.

One Day with Jesus

Copyright © 2015 by Franklin Richardson

ISBN: 978-0692571866

Unless otherwise indicated, all Scripture quotations are taken from the King James Version of the bible.

All rights reserved. No part of this book may be reproduced, stored in a retrieval system, or transmitted in any form or by any means – electronic, mechanical, photocopy, recording or any other, without permission in writing from the author,

Printed in the United States of America

Dedicated to all of our young teen adults, my son Frank, and his Youth Pastor, Clark Lund, who will face this nation's deceitfulness and morals of tomorrow.

Table of Contents

Chapter 1: *Prepare for Camp*..............................1

Chapter 2: *Arrive at Campsite*..........................20

Chapter 3: *A Father's Message*........................36

Chapter 4: *History Lesson*...............................51

Chapter 5: *The Deceiver*..................................62

Chapter 6: *The Scriptures*................................73

Author's Editorial...82

Chapter 1

Prepare for Camp

"Jim, your father wants to go camping this Saturday. He said he wants you and Frankie to get your camping stuff together and have it all ready to go. He does not want you looking for your things Saturday morning because he wants to leave early. When Frankie comes back from spending the night with Steve this morning, you two need to get out there and go through the supplies."

"Okay Mom, most of our camp stuff is ready to go. We cleaned it all up and organized it when we returned from our last campout. All we have to do is pull it out of the cabinets in the garage."

"Alright," says Mom, "I'm just letting you know. You know how your father is when he's ready to go someplace and he has to sit around and wait because we're not ready. Were you able to get that leg fixed on that one camp chair? Remember how you complained about having to sit on that big rock around the fire pit and had to keep moving it around?"

"I forgot about that. Can we go to Wal-Mart and get a new one? I tossed that one away. We can probably use a few new batteries too," says Jim.

"That's fine; just check everything before we go shopping. Make sure we have enough propane, fire logs, and any other items we may possibly need. You boys think all you need is a blanket and a sleeping bag and you're ready. Dad needs a break and he does not need to be running around to the local stores when we get out there because you boys were too lazy to make sure we had everything this time. Remember he made about five store runs last time we were out? Also bring your bible. Frank has been asking a lot of questions this week since he accepted Jesus as his personal Savior Sunday morning. This may be a good time to share Gods Word with him."

"Good idea Mom. He has already asked me a few questions about how I felt about some of the things going on in this country and around the world that have been the spotlight in the news lately. Maybe Dad can help with some of those questions. At fourteen and sixteen I think we both need a little more understanding of what's changed and how this country is becoming so out of touch with what's happening to it. I was so happy when he made that decision to accept Jesus as his personal Savior. Without God's love and understanding, I do not know how I would react to some of the things these kids are doing today in school. It's like, 'Just do what you want.' Times have changed and values and morals do not seem to exist anymore."

Mom says, "Sounds like Frankie coming in through the door. Let him know what's going on and you two need to start getting into the camping stuff out there. You have one day to get ready. Make a list of everything you may think we will need and we can go shopping tonight or sometime in the morning. Okay?"

"Hi Mom, Steve and his mom said to say hello. We had a pretty good time last night. It's nice to be on summer vacation. We had pizza last night, watched a movie and then Steve and I played video games until about three o'clock this morning. His mom got us up at seven o'clock and said we needed to have breakfast because he needed to cut the grass and clean up the yard a little bit before it got too hot outside. I helped him with hosing down the driveway. Now I can go lay back down for a few hours."

Jim says, "I don't think so. Dad wants to go camping Saturday and he was very clear to mom he wants us to have everything ready to go when he gets up. So you and I have to get into that garage and go through all the camping gear to make sure we have everything we need. You can take a nap after we finish getting everything out and organized. Okay?"

"Wow, going camping again so soon? We just went three weeks ago. Dad must be bored. He was a little upset last time because he had to run to that local store a half dozen times because we didn't have this or that," says Frankie.

"That's right, and he made it clear to Mom he does not want to do that again. So we need to start going through everything that we have and Mom will take me to Wal-Mart to get the things we need."

"Great, that sounds good to me. I love camping, I think it's relaxing and you seem to forget all the crazy things going on around you for a couple of days.

Prepare for Camp

Let me grab a sandwich and a Pepsi and we can get started."

Jim says, "While you're having a bite to eat, I will start pulling things out of the cabinets. Speaking of pizza, why don't we have that for dinner tonight? This will save time from mom having to cook tonight so she can start getting some of her things together."

"Sounds good to me, I can eat pizza every night. How about you, Mom? Will Pizza be okay? Dad likes it."

"Sure, sounds good to me. And yes, I need to start getting things ready for your father and myself too. In fact he should be home in a few hours and I'm sure he will be happy that we are getting everything ready."

(Half hour later)

Frank says, "Wow, you have everything out already. What do you want me to go through?"

"Why don't you check the box with the compasses, flashlights, water bottles and things we will need for hiking? Make sure you check all the batteries too. And don't forget the walkie-talkies. They are good for up to one mile or so. I'm sure Mom will want to check in on us every ten minutes to see where we are and what we are doing when we go on hikes. Then you can check all the cooking accessories and put those items together. Make sure we have all the pans, stove, propane, matches and cooking utensils. I will work on checking out the lanterns, clothes line, fire wood, chairs, tents, and all the other campsite items that we will need," Jim says.

Mom steps out into the garage. "Wow, look at this. You boys have just about everything laid out. Your dad is going to be one happy camper before we even leave. He should be home here shortly. He said he may come home a little earlier today. Maybe we will just go out for pizza and take a break as soon as he gets home."

Prepare for Camp

Jim says, "You act like we've never done this before. I think we pretty well have everything together, Mom. All we need now is to put a list of items together that we need to pick up at Wal-Mart. Frankie, let's clean up before Dad gets home. I guess you missed your nap, but at least we got everything together and you can sleep well tonight. I agree with Mom, Dad is going to be very surprised and happy that we have everything together already."

"Speaking of Dad, I think that's him pulling into the driveway. That was timing," says Frank.

"Hi Sweetheart, how was your day today? Did you talk to the boys about going camping Saturday?"

Mom feigns a surprised look. "What camping?"

"What do you mean, 'What camping'? I told you we were going camping Saturday and you needed to let the boys know so they can get everything ready."

Mom smiles, "I'm just kidding. The boys worked hard today and they have just about everything put together already. We are going out for pizza after you calm down for a minute and they come down from cleaning up. Let me show you what they have done."

"My goodness, look at this," says Dad. "That's my boys. It looks like they have everything ready to go. Great!"

"Hi Dad, how was your day today?"

"It was pretty good. I see you boys were quite busy today."

"Mom said you wanted everything ready by Saturday morning. Frank and I have everything ready. Mom will take me to Wal-Mart in the morning to get a few necessary items. As always, she takes care of the meals. It looks like we need a chair, propane, batteries and maybe a few items that Frank hasn't told me about yet. I was surprised when Mom said we were going this Saturday."

"It's been a crazy week, Son, and I just thought it would be nice for us just to get away this weekend and relax a little. It's only about a two hour drive to get out there. When you listen to the same negative news hour after hour, day after day, sometimes you just want to get away from it all for a couple of days. They harp on the same thing over and over again. People get tired of hearing it. All you hear about these days is discrimination, gay rights, people getting killed, bad cops and what we are going to do about ISIS.

Prepare for Camp

What's happening to this country? That's the press. Can't they talk about something good going on in this country or around the world? The only thing good that I heard on the news this week was a puppy rescued from a burning building. I get so frustrated when these people think they speak for everyone. Listen to them once in a while: 'Most of the people think this should be this way or that way.' How do they know what most of the people think? That's the problem we have today, everybody thinks they know what everybody else thinks. It's not what the people think, it's what *they* think. Don't get me started right now; I want to enjoy the night."

Jim says, "I know Dad, it's getting pretty bad out there. I was just talking to a friend of mine and we were asking similar questions. Why are these things happening and what will America be like when we are twenty-five years old? I'm almost afraid to find out."

He calls upstairs, "Frank, hurry up, it's time to go eat! We're still sitting down here waiting for you."

"I'm coming! I was looking for a couple of tapes I wanted to take with us to listen to on the way and I did not want to forget them. Hi Dad, are we just going to sit here and look at the ceiling or we going to get some pizza?"

Mom says, "Okay, let's go. Mark, would you like me to drive? I know you're a little tired."

"No that's okay; it's only up the street a few blocks."

"Guess we picked the right night to go out for pizza. Look Dad, they have a special on the spaghetti and meatball dinner. I bet that's what you're going to have. I think I'm still going for the peperoni pizza."

"That's right, Frank, that's just what I am going to have." Says Dad

Jim says, "Pizza for me too. How about you, Mom?"

"Pizza."

(An hour later)

Mom says, "Now that we are all full, we need to get home and get some things done. In the morning Jim and I will go do some shopping and Frank, you can clean up the yard a little. When Dad gets home, you boys can load up the van. This way we can have breakfast and be out on the road by 7:30 Saturday morning."

(Two hours later)

Prepare for Camp

"Dad, thanks for taking us out for pizza earlier. I think I have all my personal things together. Mom, I did pack my bible. This is a good time to go camping because the crowds will not start camp season for a few more weeks. My youth pastor says he likes to go camping before the crowds start coming in. He says he likes to explore God's creation and it gives him time to spend some quality time with the Lord. He says new Christians should spend some time with the Lord and focus on what He is doing in their lives. He says we get so caught up in homework, housework, playing with our friends and don't get to really see or hear what Jesus is doing in our lives except on Sunday mornings."

"He's right, Jim. We live in a fast-paced society today. Sometimes we just get lost and confused in what's going on around us. Often we do not focus on some of the most important things in life that we should be focusing on. When you accepted Jesus into your heart as your personal Savior, you made a commitment to Him. It's also your testimony that you believe He is the son of God and He died on that cross that your sins would be forgiven."

"I know He changed my life. It's only been a year since I accepted him as my personal Savior and He has helped me change the way I see things and live my life each day. The more I pray and read his Word, the more He reveals himself to me."

Dad says, "Jesus is awesome. He's not going to push you. He wants you to grow spiritually every day. I want you to remember one thing. As you grow and live your life so that it may be pleasing to God, He will direct your path. Many people will try to convince you that you are wrong in what you may believe when God speaks to you. Today, many people are trying to change what Gods Word means on this subject or that subject.

It's not about what they think is right or wrong, it's about what Jesus lays upon your heart. He will lead you down the path of righteousness. He will not allow Satan to have any control of your thoughts and mind because there is no place within the heart of a believer that will satisfy his glorification.

He knows the power of the words, *'Get thee behind me, Satan.'* (Matthew 16:24) He has been defeated already. In today's vocabulary what Jesus is saying is, 'Satan, don't mess with the mind of my child.' That's why it's so important to keep your thoughts and mind upon Jesus. If you're not living for Christ and your mind and thoughts are not focused on the Lord, then the deceiver has the opportunity to work on deceiving you. He can present you with things that can change your thoughts and mind to follow him. Wouldn't it be nice to spend just one day with Jesus?"

"It sure would be. Dad, do you think people change what God is saying in his Word because it's sometimes hard to live their lives around people who just don't believe? Do you think some people just give in to nonbelievers so they can avoid arguments?"

"Actually it's both. God's word is simple. Unfortunately man makes it difficult to understand. Today we have all types of religions and beliefs. Everyone wants to change Gods Word to meet their lifestyles, not his lifestyle. When I know something is wrong and I can convince you its right then I don't have to worry about it. Today it seems to be easier to give in to the nonbeliever because their voices are being heard and the believers are not speaking out in the same fashion.

Satan is strong. If you're not a strong believer in Christ he can convince you to just give up and follow him and go with the flow. That's why it's so important today to stay in God's Word and pray every day, not just once a week. When the Spirit of the Lord is within you, don't you know He will direct your path of righteousness? His Spirit will let you know when something is wrong. Look, it's getting late and we need to get some sleep."

"Thanks for the talk, Dad. See you in the morning and I can't wait to see what God has in store for us on our campout. Good night. Love you."

(Next morning)

Jim says, "You're up pretty early Mom, did you get a goodnight sleep?"

"Early? Your father had breakfast and left about an hour ago. You boys overslept this morning, it's almost 9:30. I should be ready in about another hour and we can go shopping for our supplies. Did you talk with Frank to see if there was anything you needed to add to your list?"

"Not yet, he was in the shower upstairs when I came down. We only need a few items and whatever food you want to get. We can pick up ice in the morning for the coolers. Dad and I had a good talk last night about believers and non-believers. I like talking about the Lord with him. He kind of puts things into another perspective when it comes to living your life for the Lord and it's a real eye opener."

"Your father actually has a lot of biblical knowledge. He was a youth leader years ago. He really enjoyed working with the teens. Sometimes he can give you good food for thought. When it comes to understanding God's direction for you, it may be a little challenging at times. The Lord has a plan and a purpose for each one of us. What He may be directing you to do may not be the same as it is for anyone else. If you just trust in him He will give you the knowledge and understanding of what He expects from you. We need to be patient when it comes to listening to God's Word so that when He speaks to you, then you will know it."

She sees Frank coming down the stairs. "It's about time you got down here. Did you have anything other than propane, batteries and another lounge chair that we need to pick up at the store?"

"Just some aluminum foil."

(That evening)

Mom says, "After dinner you boys can start loading up the van. Dad said put the coolers in last."

"Okay Mom, do you guys want to watch a movie tonight? I'll make some popcorn."

Mom says, "Jim said he was going to bed early. Put on a movie that Dad and I may like, we may stay up and watch it. No war movies either. Do we still have that one we watched awhile ago? I think it was Mrs. Doubtfire or something like that. That was pretty funny. I can watch that again and your dad got a big laugh out of it too."

"We still have it; I just have to find it. If I can't, we can watch something else that we all like. We need to sort those movies by titles."

(A few hours later)

Mom says, "I enjoyed that movie. It's sad that such a star like Robin Williams would commit suicide. He was such an entertainer. It's time to get some sleep; we have a long day tomorrow."

Prepare for Camp

"Okay Mom, you and Dad get some sleep too. We never get a real good night's sleep when we go camping," says Frank.

(5 o'clock in the morning)

Frank says, "I didn't sleep too much last night. I don't know about Jim, but I was laying there most of the night thinking about the campout. Did you get some sleep last night, Dad?"

"Actually I passed out within a minute after I hit that pillow. I got a good night's sleep. Let me know when you boys are ready to start loading the van. I want to get out of here as soon as we can. Honey, make sure I stop at that gas station on the corner before we get on the highway. I want to fill the coolers with ice."

Frank says, "We were going to pack last night but we watched the movie instead."

(Seven o'clock)

Frank says, "Dad we are packed and ready to go."

"Good, looks like we can get out on time. Hopefully you boys did not forget anything. I just hate getting out there and having to go back into town for some little item that we should have checked before we left. I want this to be a memorable family campout.

I like looking back at the photos of you boys on these campouts. Remember your first outing? You were about six and eight. I remember you boys wouldn't leave your mom's side. Now you just run off."

Frank says, "That's because the deer and donkey's roam around free at that campground. Remember when I had to go to the bathroom one night and you turned your flashlight on? There were seven deer about twenty feet away from our tent. That scared me because I didn't expect to see them just roaming around out there."

"I remember at your ages I didn't think to tell you about them freely roaming around. And every year we see a few of them around the camp and a few on the trails, don't we?"

"I guess if I have to get up and go, I would rather see a deer than a stranger."

"Everybody just relax and enjoy the ride," says Mom.

(Nine o'clock)

Prepare for Camp

"Looks like we are going to be right on time. We have about five miles to go, and we should be entering the campground. I would like to get the same campsite that we had a few weeks ago. It should be available at this time. The campers usually don't start coming out for another few weeks.

I think I will stop at the little store just before we go into the camp area. If anyone needs to use the restroom or pick up any snacks or whatever, now is the time to do it."

Chapter 2
Arrive at Campsite

"Well here we are, and what are the chances we would be greeted by a deer at the campsite? I think this is going to be one of those memorable trips. I am going to park the van between those two trees, just left of the picnic table. The tents can be put just right of the table, about twenty five feet back. Let's check the site out before we unload.

Jim, you and Frank can walk about a quarter of a mile around the camp while Mom and I will check all around the camp itself. If you see any trash, broken

Arrive at Campsite

glass or anything that should not be lying around, bring it back. We don't need to be tripping on things if we wander away a little during the night. It looks like the park rangers have the area pretty well cleaned up. If by chance someone may be camping close, do not cut through their camp site. Some people do not like that, just go around them."

"Okay Dad. I remember when we were here just a few weeks ago and somebody threw some beer bottles and soda cans into the fire pit next to our camp and left them. Some people just don't care about the environment; it's just about having fun to them."

"You're right. They just come out to drink and party. They're not thinking about anybody else or the park itself. That's why the fees go up, to help maintain the park.

Frank, why don't you pray for God's blessings and that He'll give us a safe outing before we get started?"

"Okay Dad. Lord, thank you for this beautiful day and for the opportunity for us to enjoy it together as a family. Please keep us safe as we take in your amazing creation. Thank you for blessing us."

Mom says, "Thanks, Frank. Now, you boys be careful out there. Remember you're not in your back yard having a cookout."

"Mom, we're not babies anymore. You need to relax, where is your faith? Frank just got done praying asking the lord to watch over us. Check the camp area out with Dad and go take a walk. We're not going to be that long. Then we can get everything unloaded and get this camp set up. Okay? Frank, are you ready? Grab some water from the cooler in the van and we can go."

"Okay, I'm ready. Let's go up this way and come around. I remember this area. Just around the bend is where the boulder overlooking the creek is. Look, there's a camper just at the bend up there. He's standing up by those boulders up there."

"I don't see him."

"Right up there. Let's stop and say hello."

"You boys need to stop right there," the stranger calls out. "About ten minutes ago I passed by there, about three feet from where you are on the path, and I noticed a five to six foot rattler coiled up right next to that log to your left. Do you see it? Now, back up slowly and come around to your right."

Arrive at Campsite

"Wow, there he is. Boy he is big isn't he? Jim move back before we startle him."

"Hi, I'm Jim and this is my brother Frank."

"Hi my name is Angel."

"We just arrived and were checking out the area. Our camp is just down a little and around that bend. Thanks for letting us know about the snake. Another foot or two and I'm sure we would have spooked it and without hesitation he would have bitten one of us. That was close. We normally carry our walking sticks but we haven't unpacked the van yet. Where is your camp?"

"I don't have a campsite; I live just up the road. I come in here and just explore its beauty and sometimes help the rangers put out food for the animals."

"Sure glad you were out here today. Well, you have a good day Angel. We have to finish checking the area and get back to our campsite. Thanks again.

See Frank, God does answer prayer. That was a pretty big rattler and another foot or so who knows what could have happened? He didn't even give a rattle to warn us that we were too close to him. I've heard they sometimes do not give a warning, they just strike out. Can you see Mom's face if we brought that back to camp?"

Frank says, "I don't think she would be a happy camper. That was a pretty nice guy back there and he just so happened to be at the right place at the right time. Thank you, Jesus. This afternoon we can come back up this way and climb those boulders back there to check out the small creek on the other side of them."

"Sounds good; just make sure we bring our walking sticks this time."

Arrive at Campsite

"There's Dad raking around the fire pit; looks like he has most of the stuff unpacked already."

"What took you boys so long? Your dad already started getting things set up."

Frank says, "Mom, we've only been gone for about a half hour or so. If you were with us you would have had a heart attack. We were within just a few steps from this big old rattler when we heard this man yell out to us to stop. He told us where the snake was coiled and we backed up and went around it. We didn't get to talk with him much. Jim told him we had to finish checking out the area and get back to camp."

"You boys are okay, aren't you?"

"Yes Mom, we're okay and we need to help Dad get the rest of the stuff out of the van and get this camp area set up. It looks like Dad is already clearing the brush out from around the fire pit. Let me ask him what he wants us to stark working on next.

Dad, do you want us to start putting the tents up or get Mom's kitchen set up first?"

"Can you boys start working on the tents? I want to rake a little around the area that we are going to set up the stove and set the coolers out. You can also hang the lanterns on the two trees by the eating table and one on the tree in front of the tents."

"Jim, let's finish unloading and get the tents put up."

(*One hour later*)

Jim says, "Well, it looks like we got the camp pretty well set up. If there were any little critters in the area I'm sure they've left by now with all the activity around here. Anybody want a soda?"

Mom says, "While you're taking a break I will make some sandwiches. I'm sure you're all getting a little hungry. I know Dad's going to take a little nap in the tent. What are you boys going to be doing?"

"Frank wants to go check out the creek after lunch. Want to go hike with us?"

"No, your dad and I will take a little hike around the area later on. You boys just go on and have a good time. Please be careful and stay out of trouble. Make sure you have plenty of water with you too."

"Mom, we know what we are doing; this is not our first campout. And we're not going to be that far away."

(*After lunch*)

Arrive at Campsite

"Ready Jim? I put the walking sticks by the tree. I also filled the canteens, so I think we have plenty of water."

"I've been ready. Let's go. Mom, we will be back in a couple hours. Do you need anything done before we leave?"

"No, you boys go and have a good time. I think I'm just going to sit and relax and read a book."

Dad pokes his head out of the tent and says, "You boys have a good time. Before you leave, put the coolers over by the table out of the sun and if you don't mind put the firewood by the pit."

The boys finish their chores and start out on their hike.

"Jim, I'm going to climb up on that boulder and take a picture of the creek from up there."

"Okay." A few minutes pass by.

"Frank, what are you doing up there?"

(*No response*)

"Frank, I can't see you up there. What are you doing?"

"Jim! Jim!" Frank yells out.

Jim starts to climb up the side of the boulder and notices Frank walking around the base of it. "What happened to you?"

"I was standing on the edge, getting ready to take a picture, and my foot accidently hit a small pocket and all of a sudden I fell off. You won't believe what happened. You remember that man Angel? He had just broken open about six bales of hay for the deer at the base of the boulder on the other side and I landed right in the middle of it. He was getting ready to leave as I fell off. He asked if I was okay and I told him I was fine. He said, 'Be a little more careful,' and went on his way."

Arrive at Campsite

"That's about a twenty-five foot drop."

"I know; it scared me half to death when I lost my balance. That's twice that man happened to be at the right place at the right time. That was a miracle. Thank you, Jesus."

"Do you want to continue up to the creek?"

"Of course; I didn't get a picture of it. I'm fine. It actually was a soft landing. I just sat there for a few seconds wondering about what just happened."

"Did you hear that? It sounded like some motorcycles in the background? We may have some more campers coming in. Glad Dad got his spot first. He really likes that particular campsite."

"I heard them. I hope they stay on the other side of the camp. Last time we had a few of them near our camp, they came in and out all night long."

"They make so much noise that it's hard to get any sleep. Let's get our sticks and keep going."

Frank says, "Well, there's the creek. Let's make our way down to the base of it and take a break."

(Half an hour later)

"Now this is what I call camping. Just getting away from the city and enjoying the quiet and beautiful scenery of some of God's creations. It's so peaceful out here. Some of those trees are pretty tall. I wonder how far this creek goes around, and where it ends up. I bet there are some good fish in here too. It also looks like it would be a good spot for deer crossings. Did you get enough pictures?"

Frank says, "I think so. We probably need to be heading back soon. We've been up and down this creek for a while now. Wow, where did that bottle come from? It almost hit me in the head."

Jim says, "It's those two bikers up on the trail. It looks like they are going to come down here. They probably want to mess with us. Let's head up the creek."

"Wait a minute," Frank says. "Someone just pulled up and they're going back up to talk to him. Look, they're riding away. Thank you, Jesus. Isn't that Mr. Angel waving down at us? Now he's leaving."

Jim says, "I think we should be heading back to camp now. Wait until Mom hears about what happened to us today. The first thing she's going to say is, 'Why did you leave without taking the walkie-talkies with you so you could have communicated to us?' I forgot about them until we were already at the boulder area. Boy, it's been some day!"

"You know, it's amazing how God takes care of his children. I was a little scared when those bikers started to come down. Then it was like the Lord was speaking to me and telling me, 'Fear not for my angels are watching over you.'"

"You're right; the scriptures do tell us in Isaiah 41:10, *'Fear not, for I am with you; be not dismayed, for I am your God; I will strengthen you, I will help you, I will uphold you with my righteous right hand.'*

You know what? I didn't think about it, but that man we met named Angel could have been one of Gods angels watching over us today. In Hebrews 1-7 and also in Psalm 34 the bible tells us that angels are commanded by God to 'encamp all around us' and keep us from falling or getting hurt and they have been with us and will be with us '…from this time forth and forever.' Dad was just talking about keeping your mind focused on Jesus and what it might be like just to spend one day with him."

"I think I can tell him what it would be like. I feel like I've just spent one day with Jesus. Let's get back to camp. Wait until Mom hears about my fall and the bikers. She may not let us go out again without her and Dad."

"Let's cross the creek over there and go around. Last time we were here, I wanted to get a few pictures but I didn't have my camera. Are you ready? Let's go."

"Jim, look over there by the big rocks. It's a couple of wild mules. Let's get a picture of them. Come on, walk around to the right. They don't spook too much, as long as you don't run at them or throw anything. They will just walk around and head away from you."

Arrive at Campsite

Jim says, "Let me get a picture before they turn around and start heading off." He snaps the picture. "Got it; now let's move away and let them be."

"That was pure luck coming up on those two mules. That will be a nice picture to frame if it took. The sun was pretty bright behind them."

Jim says, "Look, there they go. Let's go up through here. I know just before we get back to camp, there are a few areas I want to get some more pictures. Every time we come here we encounter or see something different. I guess that's why Dad likes to come here so much."

"I like it here. It's just like our youth pastor said. He likes exploring and spending time with the Lord when he camps. Over there looking down at the site could be another good area for some more pictures."

(*Half an hour later*)

Jim says, "There's the campsite and I sure could use a little rest. We've been gone awhile."

As the boys approach camp Mom says, "It's about time you boys got back. You forgot your walkie-talkies. And I was getting a little worried about you two. I don't care how old you are. Dad had to make a store run because he didn't think we had enough fire wood, and he did not find any large pieces lying around the area. He said there was a Spanish man there who was short about seventy cents to get a few items. He was telling the store clerk he hadn't cashed his check yet. Dad gave him a few dollars to hold him over until he gets his check cashed. Dad was talking to the man and telling him about you two and he said he thought he met you boys on the trail this morning based on Dad's description of the two of you. He was so nice and thankful that a stranger helped him out. I think he said his name was Angel.

I guess I better start getting dinner ready. We have Italian sausage, steaks or hamburgers, so let me know what you want me to pull out. I'll prep the food and Dad can cook it."

Jim says, "We both want two Italian sausages and Dad wants one of those steaks for dinner. I'll put a pan by the grill for some baked beans."

Mom says, "Honey, I think everyone is ready to eat. Go ahead and start the grill. I'll get the food ready."

"Okay," says Dad.

Chapter 3
A Father's Message

Dad says, "I got the fire started. Did everyone have enough to eat? If so, I want to discuss a few things with you boys that may be helpful in your walk as a Christian."

Mom says, "You boys never mentioned how your afternoon went. Did you have a nice outing?"

"Actually it was a really great day other than Frank slipping off the bolder he climbed. It was about a twenty five foot drop. And not to mention, also running into a couple of bikers."

"What?"

"Mom, relax. He landed in a pile of hay. That man Angel helps the park rangers feed the animals and he just finished putting out some hay at the base of that boulder and Frank landed right into it. He also happened to pull up just as those bikers were coming down to the creek. He talked with them and they left. The rest of the day was great.

We ran into a couple wild mules and took some pictures and then we started back in. We thought Angel was an angel that God put there to watch over us today."

"Was that the same man that told you about that snake?"

"It sure was."

"Well, God bless that man. You boys could have gotten hurt pretty badly and who knows what those bikers would have done with nobody around?

I think you boys need to take your father along if you're going that far away. I'm sure your father knows that verse in the bible that says, '*Keep on loving one another as brothers and sisters. Do not forget to show hospitality to strangers, for by so doing some people have shown hospitality to angels without knowing it.'"*

"You know if we take Dad, you go too. He's not about to leave you alone."

Mom just turns away, looks up and says, "Lord thank you for watching over my boys, and thank you for Angel. Let this be a lesson that they will remember the rest of their lives on how you bless and watch over your children if they just put their trust in you. Amen."

As Dad sits down he says, "I want to talk to you a little about some of the things you may be seeing or hearing about in the news lately. These things can affect the way you may live your life. I was a little upset hearing some of the news this week. That's why I wanted to just get away from it all, relax and do some thinking. What I want to talk about are things that can cause you to change the way you may respond to situations or things that you may not agree with. As Christians you want to be very careful on how you speak and react to others.

Our society has changed. People are not as compassionate like they used to be. Today so many are out to hurt and destroy anything that once represented something good that took place in this nation. They want to remove monuments, take away rights, and destroy individual's lives and anything to do with American culture or values. In their eyes they have to destroy the memories of the old America in order to build what they call a 'New America.' They quickly respond to any opportunity to destroy with no time for problem solving or looking at options that may be a better way to address issues.

I guarantee it, five years from now the American people will be living in one of the most unwanted countries in the world if they don't wake up and discontinue on the path they are currently taking. It could be just a year or two, who knows? Keep your eyes on what the government will do in the coming years that will strip your rights to your beliefs in Christ. Eventually they will put you in prison for standing up for your beliefs in Christ.

You know why? We, the people, allow it to happen. We continue to just go with the flow. This group wants this; this group wants that. We don't like this; we don't like that, fine. The government that we, the people, elected, give them what they want.

We have no time today to stop and think or come up with solutions that may benefit the majority of the people. Sadly, the ones with the loudest voices seem to just get what they want.

We open our doors to this country to thousands of refugees and other individuals across the world. They come in and after a period of time, they choose to become citizens of this great nation. Unfortunately they bring their own culture and religious beliefs with them. All of a sudden they have a right to practice their spiritual beliefs. I have no problem with that. Everyone believes in something, or somebody that they worship.

I do have a problem when they continue to move here and continue pushing the American way of life to the wayside. And try to implement their ideas and culture to replace ours. They feel they should not have to look at crosses on your mountain tops. They do not need to pass by the symbols of your Ten Commandments, and their children should not have to take an active role in reciting your Pledge of Allegiance.

Well, let's pass a law that does not require you to recite our Pledge of Allegiance in a classroom if its offensive to you and you do not believe the Almighty God as we do.

We pass too many laws that are not properly addressing the American people. It's all about the voices of power.

Eisenhower stated 'From this day forward, the millions of our school children will daily proclaim in every city and town, every village and rural school house, the dedication of our nation and our people to the Almighty... In this way we are reaffirming the transcendence of religious faith in America's heritage and future; in this way we shall constantly strengthen those spiritual weapons which forever will be our country's most powerful resource, in peace or in war.'

Take this away, and we ask ourselves the question, 'What's happened to America?' They say, 'Don't even worry about it, we will be just fine.'

Why are these terrorist running around America pulling their comrades together to kill in the name of whomever? Think about it.

It reminds me of a song by Johnny Cash, 'One Piece at a Time.' We are falling apart one piece at a time. After a period of time, what do we have? Nothing.

I have to be very careful on how I present this to you. I do not want you to think all these people are the same. We have a lot of beautiful people living here from many different countries. I have friends that are Spanish, African-American, Indian, and Muslim. My concern is when you have a group of them that feel they speak for all of them. They make sure their voices are heard, and so we jump to accommodate them. Then when something goes wrong, we blame all of them.

This is America. If you do not like our way of life, leave. Look how many people judged Mr. Trump on his point of view when he spoke about the Mexican people coming across our boarders.

He said we are getting all their thieves, drug dealers, and murderers and so on. Because he did not address all the good folks living here from there, he was criticized.

His point was the American people have had enough, and we need to put a stop to it. He was addressing border issues. I'm sure he knows we have thousands of good Mexican folks living in this nation. This is not to say I would or would not vote for him. He speaks the truth and he will not back down. That's the problem we have today in America. We need a person who will take a stand and hear the voice of the people. Our leaders are not too concerned about us anymore. We need new leadership that will take a stand and defend the rights of the American people.

Please understand, there will always be two sides to everything. Everybody wants to be right and nobody wants to be wrong. That's normal; that's why we live in a nation where we elect officials to help us to make the right choices. Unfortunately, they have been unable to make any common sense decisions that would benefit all of the people; at least not lately.

This is going to cause even more friction across this nation if they do not change the way they manage government decisions. A good example would be those two drunken bikers throwing a beer bottle at you and then wanting to come down to possibly hurt you. Someone with authority talked with them and they left. Do you know what would have happened if they would have found your bodies lying dead by the creek?

A few hundred people would say they should not allow bikers into the campsites. Do you really think that's going to stop people like them from coming in without bringing their beer and conducting criminal activities? I don't think so. The ones that are going to lose out are those social bikers who just want to enjoy themselves and have a beer or two. The issue wasn't the bikes; it was the criminal mindset of the men committing the crime whether they were on motorcycles or in a vehicle. There are a lot of crazy people out there.

What they need to do is put more security in the campgrounds, not take away the bikers' rights to enjoy the environment like everyone else. If it's not a safe place for people to be because they cannot make it safe enough, then close it down to all, not just a few.

Our leaders are just making quick decisions today to quiet down a few individuals who feel they have the right answers for this nation's problems. A few individuals are not speaking for the majority of the people. It's about what the majority of American people think is right.

What about the rest of us who have to live with these quick decisions? Our elected officials need to slow down and take a good look at what's best for the nation as a whole, not just a few who let their voices be heard.

By not slowing down and getting a full understanding to address issues in a manner that they should, they're going to cause chaos across this nation. This is why it's even more important today to live your life focused on Jesus. I was so happy when you said you just spent one day with Jesus. Can you imagine what it would feel like if you spent your whole life with him?

I know some of the things I am going to talk about are more for the adults, but somewhere down the line it will affect the way you may live your life. Our youth today will be our leaders tomorrow. The adults think like children today. Quick responses, dumb laws, and having no clue to why this nation is falling apart are proof of that.

When I hear that children's song, 'Jesus Loves the Little Children of the World,' I think of the adults running our country today. I know the majority of people in America do not love them for what they have done to this nation.

Let me give you an example of how something can be interpreted if seen or heard by someone who does not have a full understanding of what they may have seen or heard and then voice their opinion. I know you boys know all about sex.

I had a friend who was working one night and it was almost midnight. He was walking with another employee and a young lady friend came along and said, 'Sam, I need a quick jump again tonight. I get off in about fifteen minutes.' He said, 'Okay. Meet me in front of the building and I will drive us to the back of the building. I'll try to get you out of here as soon as I can.' She said 'Great, I don't want my husband to worry about me if I get home to late.' Then the coworker says, 'Wow, I didn't know you were messing around with Mary.'

Sam said, 'I'm not messing around with her.'

The coworker said, 'Sure, I know what I just heard. She needs you to jump her tonight. I also saw you go behind the back of the parking lot a couple times this week. Don't worry, I won't tell anybody what you guys are doing.'

What do you think is going on?"

Frank says, "Sounds like she is sexually active and she does not want her husband to find out she's having an affair."

"What about you, Jim?"

"Well most of the guys at school are always saying, "Boy she looks good. I think I really want to jump her some night. But she's taken already."

"So that's what you boys think is going on?"

Frank says, "I know what you're going to say. 'That's not what Jesus would have us do.'"

"You're right, that's not what Jesus would want us to do if that were the case. But that's not the case here. Sam jumped her battery three times that week because it was going bad and she asked him again."

Jim says, "You're kidding me. Wow, we were missing something."

"If she said, 'Sam, I need you to jump my battery again tonight, there would have been no concern at all. This is why we should not just jump to conclusions when people complain about this and that without a little thought into what's being seen or heard.

People can get hurt. A few words missed or a misunderstanding of them can be very hurtful or damaging. Actually if I did not say to you before I spoke, 'I know you boys know all about sex,' you would have probably taken a little time to think about what really was going on. Putting that in your thought pattern was basically saying something sexually was going on. Are you getting the point?"

Frank says, "You're right. I thought it was going to be something about sex."

"One of the biggest issues being talked about across our nation today is discrimination. That's a big word, and it should be. I would venture to say the majority of this nation's problems are due to discrimination in one form or another. When you have a problem this big, you're not going to change it overnight by making radical quick decisions to try and diffuse it. If the government itself discriminates against a select group of people, do you think they're going to make the correct decision to fix the problem?"

"What do you mean by that, Dad?"

A Father's Message

"What I mean by that is our law makers are pushing out so many laws they think are beneficial to people's best interests, but unfortunately they start hurting the citizens. The majority of us live our lives based on our constitutional rights. We put our trust in God and our trust in our federal appointed leaders. This is what makes us a great nation. Do you know what our national flag represents?

It represents liberty and justice for all. When we talk about our pledge of allegiance to this flag it's not just for the whites, the blacks, the natives, the rich or its politicians. When we as Americans give our allegiance to this flag, it represents *all* Americans in the republic; all states, not just twenty of them. The poor along with the rich, all races not just two, and most importantly, it represents all the people not just ninety five percent of them.

This nation is in one accord, and I'm not speaking about a little car that has four individuals in it. That's what I think some of our leaders think. When you make a pledge to something, it's because you believe in it. You are expressing allegiance to what you believe it represents.

Did you know our pledge of allegiance has been rewritten three times already?"

Jim says, "I didn't know that."

"Well you should if you pledge an allegiance to it. Do you even know what an allegiance to your flag means?

"I believe it signifies your commitment and loyalty to the way your country expects you to live, according to the laws governing this country," says Jim.

"Pretty close. When I was in grade school they never explained the meaning of the pledge of allegiance to the flag. They just had you memorize it so as a whole you could all say it together, whether you understood its meaning or not. Hopefully today they are teaching you what that allegiance means as well as the true meanings of the words put in it."

Frank says, "They still do not teach us that. We just memorize it and do the same thing you did."

"You're kidding me. This is another good reason you need to keep God's Word in your heart. You get a very clear understanding of what his Word means.

Tonight we are going to have a discussion on what that flag and your allegiance to it mean. Let's start from the beginning."

Chapter 4

History Lesson

Mark takes his notes out of his bible and arranges them in front of him.

"The Pledge of Allegiance has changed over time. At one point in time it said, '*I pledge allegiance to my Flag and the Republic for which it stands, one nation, indivisible, with liberty and justice for all.*'

In 1923, the words changed. They added 'the flag of the United States of America.' Now it says, '*I pledge allegiance to the Flag of the United States of*

America and to the Republic for which it stands, one nation, indivisible, with liberty and justice for all.'

In 1954, when I was a little boy, they changed it again. Congress added the words, 'under God' to it. Now it says, *'I pledge allegiance to the flag of the United States of America, and to the republic for which it stands, one nation under God, indivisible, with liberty and justice for all.'*

I remember my father talking about this one. They finally acknowledged God. To him allegiance and trust were just about the same. Who knows where this country would be if they did not trust in God? When we put God aside, this nation will surely feel the hand of evil. We put our trust in words that make an impact on the way we will live our lives. If they are just words that have no real meaning then why would one trust or give his allegiance to them?

Now that you understand how we ended up with the pledge of allegiance as it reads today, let's see if you understand the meaning of key words that people put their faith and trust in. It took a president that had values and stood for the people. We find it pretty hard to find men to lead this nation today that want to take a stand for the people and the God we used to trust in. Look at the turmoil that's going on

History Lesson

across this nation. Do you really believe it just happen by coincidence?

Eisenhower signed the bill into law on Flag Day, June 14, 1954. He stated 'From this day forward, the millions of our school children will daily proclaim in every city and town, every village and rural school house, the dedication of our nation and our people to the Almighty.... In this way we are reaffirming the transcendence of religious faith in America's heritage and future; in this way we shall constantly strengthen those spiritual weapons which forever will be our country's most powerful resource, in peace or in war.'

Now keep in mind these words apply to every man, woman and child that are citizens of this nation, not just a few, but to all. As Christians we have no problem with understanding why they used the words 'under God.' God's words are true. When He speaks to you, He speaks the truth. He is not a God that will deceive you or change words that will cause confusion like man does.

What does the word *indivisible* mean? Some definitions from Webster's dictionary are:

1. United and can't be broken up or divided.
2. Cannot be split up.
3. Rock solid.

What does the word *liberty* mean? Here are a few definitions:

1. The condition of being free from confinement, servitude or forced labor.
2. The condition of being free from oppression restriction or control.

What about the word *justice*? What does it mean?

1. The quality of being just: fairness.
2. Treat everyone the same.
3. The principal of moral rightness, decency and conformity.

It's hard to believe our leadership today does not have a clear sense of direction on where they are taking this nation. We're not blind; we just can't face the truth. The rich do not care about what's happening and they are living in a fantasyland. It's the poor and weary who are going to feel and see the impact first when this nation fails to live up to its old values which we once lived by.

History Lesson

Hopefully you boys now have a better understanding of why you pledge your allegiance to your nation's flag. It's not something you should take lightly. It's not something you memorize, but something you live by.

Earlier we talked about discrimination and how I feel the government makes decisions against what is wrong for the people yet today they themselves commit discrimination to a few because they are allowed to create civil right acts that say they can. They must have just memorized the Pledge of Allegiance too. Just like many others, they have no idea of what the words mean.

Unfortunately the truth speaks for itself. Do you remember your grandmother was terminated because her employer wanted young ladies working for him?

She was able to prove that she lost her employment at age sixty-two because of age discrimination."

Jim says, "Yes, I remember that. They said she could not file for age discrimination even if she could prove it because the company has to have more than fifteen employees in order for the law to take effect. If they had sixteen employees, then she could have filed a complaint and taken them to court. Grandma really had a rough time raising little Tommy without a job. She had to move to a small house, change his school, cut his activities and was unable to give him a vacation. It really upset her when she had to apply for early social security just to make ends meet. She said that if this nation continues to allow these types of laws to govern its citizens because one person feels it is right, then it's wrong. I agree, Dad, that's not fair for the elderly to pay for protecting small businesses."

Dad says, "Wait a minute, didn't we just go over why we give our allegiance to our national flag based on our interpretation of its meaning when it comes to living our lives in this great nation? I think I missed a very important word."

"What word is that, Dad?"

"The word...*all*.

History Lesson

Think about this. Let's look at what the word *all* really means:

1. Representing the entire or total number.
2. Completely, fully and totally.
3. Everyone, everybody.

It looks like the state of Arizona and a few others overlooked the meaning of a couple words, when it comes to discrimination. What happened to the words *'justice for all?'* Where is the justice for those elderly folks being discriminated against because they're not protected by the law according to what we understand? What happened to the meaning of indivisible, which is 'cant split up?'

(*Justice for all*)

I guess we should write a letter to Congress and ask them to change the wording again to '*I pledge allegiance to the flag of the United States of America, and to the republic for which it stands, one nation under God, with liberty and justice for some.*'

What are we missing here? It plainly says it's unlawful for employment practices to discriminate against *any individual* because of race, color, religion, sex and age 40 years or older. My understanding is that *any individual means all.* It seems I forgot that this is the new America. The next part of that law basically says it's okay to discriminate as long as the company employs less than fifteen employees. If the employer has more than sixteen employees then it is not allowed and they can face charges for age discrimination. To me that's discriminating to those fifteen individuals by eliminating the so-called *justice for all.*

That's like telling the black folks who are taking the blunt of discrimination today, 'Look you cannot file for discrimination protection if you have less than 200 black people in your city. If your city has 201 black folks then you may qualify for applying for justice in accordance to the civil rights laws governing our State (Civil rights Act 101b).

History Lesson

What happened to our rights to believe we cannot be split-up or have restrictions put on us and that everybody is treated the same according to our allegiance to the flag that represents the true meaning of our freedom?

Boys, these are serious issues that we face today. To me it's not a joke. But talking to individuals today reveals that is exactly how they are starting to feel about the way our leaders are running our government today. And this is just one subject. I don't even want to get into it about the people who are over-running our nation and who do not believe in the God that we at once trusted in according to the Holy Bible. Christ is being removed to open the door to the gods of deception.

This is how the actual law reads: '*The Arizona Civil Rights Act makes it an unlawful employment practice to discriminate against any individual because of race, color, religion, sex, age (40 years old or older), national origin or disability. Employers with fifteen or more employees during twenty or more weeks of the current or preceding calendar year are covered by the Act.*'

Do you think discrimination is going to stop, if the lawmakers themselves are allowed to do it? They know what they are doing. They are protecting small business rights over the people's rights. We need to look at the justice system to ensure all are treated equal not just the majority.

It's like the law makers are playing games with our rights today. I'm just adding a little humor here, but this is the way a lot of citizens feel today:

'Hey lawmaker, I have a small business that I would like to open, I was wondering what you can do for me if I open one of my businesses in your state?'

'Let's see, we have the *Lets make a Deal* game.'

'What's that?'

'We change the age discrimination law that protects your interest, and take it away from some of the people, not all mind you, just enough to protect your rights as a business partner. Okay?'

'Because most small businesses have less than fifteen employees, we will modify that law, and add a Civil Rights Act that will not allow up to fifteen people to take you to court if you violate any age discrimination laws. If you go over that number, we cannot protect your business. What do you think of

History Lesson

that? Let's make a deal. Push the red button to make a deal or push the black button if there is no deal.'

'What about sexual harassment?'

'Sorry, we cannot cut the numbers on that one. Everyone is covered, even if you just have one employee. What's it going to be, deal or no deal?'

'Deal. I like this state. You see justice one way while the people see it another; and you just ignore it.'

'Welcome to Arizona. If you're rich and powerful, it's no big deal. The only buttons we push are the people living under this new Civil rights Act. Just remember to keep your employee number under fifteen or you'll have trouble. Have a nice day.'"

Chapter 5
The Deceiver

Dad says, "I've talked about one subject tonight that affects everyone's life. When we come back, I would like to talk a little about the deceiver, Satan."

(*Half an hour later*)

Dad says, "Did everyone have a nice break? I know it's getting a little late, so I think I will talk about a few other topics that this nation is facing when we get back home. Right now I want to talk about how Satan is deceiving so many people today and it is causing so much hurt and bitterness across our country.

We talked about our flag and its meaning. What about the words *'In God we Trust?'* I believe its meaning is that we put our trust in the one and only God who, at one point, we believed to be the Father, Son and Holy Spirit based on our beliefs in the Holy Bible. The Holy Bible is the Word of God. You cannot change God's Word to conform to what you may feel is right and moral just so it will fit your lifestyle.

This is what Christianity faces today. Satan has deceived so many individuals into believing that Christ is not the Son of God. God himself says He is, and through him, and only thru him, will you enter the Kingdom of God. That's pretty plain to me.

That's where people draw the line today. They take a few verses and start to change them to meet their own beliefs and not what the real meaning or true intent of the Scriptures are.

What we need today is for our youth to take a stand and reach out to all the young. They need to face today, not yesterday. Our world has changed.

Let God do his battles. He is very capable. What He wants you to do is love one another and tell them about salvation and God's love for them. It's not our place to judge or condemn. Put your trust in God, not man. Sharing and showing his love is what can change the hearts of many of these individuals.

Many people know no other way except for the way they were raised. Religion and faith typically come from your parents' traditional beliefs. If this is what someone was taught from birth, it will be very hard to find something else that may be acceptable to them if this was the foundation that their parents instilled in them.

This is one example of Satan's strongholds on many individuals today. As Christians all we can do is continue reaching out to them and show them God's love for them.

One day their hearts may open to hear the voice of the Lord speaking to them. Hopefully it will not be too late. God's Word is much more powerful than the deceiver.

The Deceiver

Let's take a few moments to talk about the terrorist group, ISIS. These people have caused havoc around the world for all people, but especially for Muslims. Just like we in America have our spiritual beliefs, they, in their region, have their beliefs. Unfortunately, when a group like this achieves such notoriety for evil, the world looks at all Muslims and believes they hold the same beliefs. It's not true. I know a lot of Muslims and they are beautiful, kind and wonderful people. We all want to promote our own religious beliefs. When you have a group that in the name of their god needs to kill and murder innocent women and children and bring destruction upon the earth, you can see they have been deceived. I call this group ISIS: *Insane, Satanic, Individual Servants* terrorizing the real Muslim people.

These people clearly are cowards as they hide behind woman and children. They are not soldiers, they're a bunch of gun-toting terrorist that claim to serve the god that many Muslims believe in. When you see a Muslim you may think 'terrorist.' That's what the deceiver wants you to believe. These people are servants of the deceiver who is Satan. The god this group serves is not the God that most Muslims worship. They worship a loving God as we do. We just have different beliefs. You boys have a lot of Muslims in your school, so you love them and be kind to them just as your God would want you to.

There are many different religions and people can worship as they please. Only God can change the heart of man. Someday they may have a different point of view and a change of heart when it comes to the Scriptures.

Jesus himself had to deal with Satan. Because of this, I believe He knows what we face on a daily basis and He protects us from this deceiver. It's like a battle every day. Satan cannot battle Gods Word and be victorious, unless you change his Word to mean something else. Satan himself believed that Jesus was the son of God, otherwise why would he even try to deceive and tempt him? Let's see what happened. Honey, hand me my bible sitting on the cooler next to you." She hands him the bible. "Thank you. Let's see what the Scriptures say about Satan's temptations. I also have a few notes that I copied concerning this topic.

'And the devil said unto Him, if thou be the Son of God, command this stone that it be made bread.' (Luke 4:3)

Jesus was now at his weakest. He had just fasted for forty days. We may note the first temptation involves food. It comes in the form of a challenge, '*if thou be*' then prove it by doing this or that. We may say, 'This sounds reasonable. After all, Jesus was hungry.' This temptation certainly would have appealed to his flesh. What really was at stake here was this: Would Jesus be led by the Spirit of God? Or would He be led by the devil?

Would Jesus follow and obey God? Or would He follow and obey the devil? Jesus is the Son of God. He had the power to turn the rocks into bread. However, it needs to be noted that doing so would not have been the will of the Father, but rather what Satan desired him to do. This temptation was also devoted to 'self.' He was being tempted to satisfy his hunger by using his divine power. The miracles that Jesus later did benefited others, not himself. Satan wanted Jesus to act independently from his Father. Should Jesus have been disobedient in even the smallest matter, He would not have been obedient in all things, even unto death.

When temptations come on you and you consider it is the devil tempting you, then you may hear in your thoughts, 'It is not the devil. It is only my own thoughts giving me some good advice.' In other cases you may hear, 'This is God speaking to me to do this or that.' But remember this verse: *'And marvel; for Satan himself is transformed into an angel of light.'* (2 Corinthians 11:14)

So, how can we discern between the thoughts that come from God and the thoughts that come from Satan?

The answer is by God's Word; study, study, and study. Get to know the voice of God from the Bible so well that you can identify the deceptions of the devil when they come. God's Word is the key. Many say, in this generation of deception we are now in, 'God told me to do this, or that,' yet it contradicts God's written Word. Beware.

Remember, Eve was also tempted with food. Jesus overcame this temptation. He did not yield to Satan's subtle deception. Jesus responded with God's Word. The way to fight Satan when he speaks to us or tempts us in our thoughts, through our flesh, or in our emotions, is by using God's Word. Jesus said, *'It is written, that man shall not live by bread alone, but by every word of God.'* (Luke 4:4) He was quoting from a passage found in Deuteronomy 8:3. Quoting God's Word to Satan caused him to cease this temptation and go on to another.

Consider what Jesus had said. His Word tells every born-again Christian how to live. We are to *Live by every word of God.* We are to live by the Bible.

Sometimes we have problems knowing where to look in the Bible for truths that help us grow. What I want you boys to do is begin reading more Christian books and using Christian sites on the internet to find the answers that may help you with your walk with Christ.

Today we have many Christians who write excellent books to help us get a better understanding of the Scriptures. They write these books because they are concerned about your spiritual life. Put a copy of some of their writing into your Bibles. Just like you've seen tonight, they've helped me in discussing certain subjects of God's Word.

As you talk with your friends you will have suggestions to help them. We are living in a day of deception and Christ is the only answer. Some books may not be written by real believers and can deceive you into believing something that is not of God. Always remember that the Holy Spirit dwells within you. Pray that God reveals the truth as you read. Jesus said, *'I am the way and the truth and the life. No man comes to the father except through me.'* (John 14:6)

Let Jesus be your strong hand against Satan. If his Spirit dwells within you, then his words are within you. Satan's only goal is to deceive you into denying Christ as your personal Savior and taking you to the pits of hell with him. It's your choice.

Accept Christ as your personal savior or be deceived and follow Satan to the pits of hell. You basically only have two choices. If you choose Jesus, you will face friends and individuals who will not agree with you when it comes to your understanding of the Word of God. You do not want to harden your heart and get angry or upset with them because they will not listen. This is what Satan wants you to do. Do not judge or condemn those that attack your beliefs.

Just do as Jesus would. Have compassion and love for them and just continue to tell them about Gods love and his way of salvation that they may be saved. One day they may have a change of heart and listen. This is what Jesus would have you do.

Look at the condition of our nation today because we have changed what we used to believe in. We have changed the meanings of things in order to conform to the few who want to destroy America. Satan is hard at work today trying to destroy the morals and values of America.

Look at what's going on in the world today. Let's see what the scriptures have to say."

Chapter 6

The Scriptures

"As Christians, we should not be surprised at what we are seeing or hearing about around the world today. The Scriptures foretold what will happen in the end times. We are seeing these Scriptures come to pass.

It should be an eye-opener for the believer, knowing that the Lord is getting close to his return for his church. Let's take a look at what the Bible tells us to be looking for at the end of time. It looks like He has given us the knowledge and understanding of what to expect. The only thing God will not reveal to us is the hour that he will return. Let's read in Matthew 24 to get a better understanding:

¹ And Jesus went out, and departed from the temple: and his disciples came to him for to shew him the buildings of the temple.

² And Jesus said unto them, See ye not all these things? Verily I say unto you, there shall not be left here one stone upon another that shall not be thrown down.

³ And as he sat upon the Mount of Olives, the disciples came unto him privately, saying, tell us, when shall these things be? And what shall be the sign of thy coming, and of the end of the world?

Dad says, "When we get closer to the Lord's return, man is going to try and confuse and deceive you. It's so important to keep his Word within our hearts. He also said that as we hear of some of these things to not be troubled by them. These things must come to pass. All these things we are seeing today are

The Scriptures

bringing so much sorrow across the world, but this is still not going to be the end…yet.

Frank, I want you to read the rest of this chapter. I think it will sink in more if you read it aloud yourself."

"Okay, Dad."

⁴ And Jesus answered and said unto them, Take heed that no man deceive you.

⁵ For many shall come in my name, saying, I am Christ; and shall deceive many.

⁶ And ye shall hear of wars and rumors of wars: see that ye be not troubled: for all these things must come to pass, but the end is not yet.

⁷ For nation shall rise against nation, and kingdom against kingdom: and there shall be famines, and pestilences, and earthquakes, in diver's places.

⁸ All these are the beginning of sorrows.

⁹ Then shall they deliver you up to be afflicted, and shall kill you: and ye shall be hated of all nations for my name's sake.

¹⁰ *And then shall many be offended, and shall betray one another, and shall hate one another.*

¹¹ *And many false prophets shall rise, and shall deceive many.*

¹² *And because iniquity shall abound, the love of many shall wax cold.*

¹³ *But he that shall endure unto the end, the same shall be saved.*

Frank says, "Wow, a lot is going to happen isn't it?"

¹⁴ *And this gospel of the kingdom shall be preached in all the world for a witness unto all nations; and then shall the end come.*

¹⁵ *When ye therefore shall see the abomination of desolation, spoken of by Daniel the prophet, stand in the holy place, (whoso readeth, let him understand :)*

¹⁶ *Then let them which be in Judaea flee into the mountains:*

17 Let him which is on the housetop not come down to take anything out of his house:

18 Neither let him which is in the field return back to take his clothes.

19 And woe unto them that are with child, and to them that give suck in those days!

20 But pray ye that your flight be not in the winter, neither on the Sabbath day:

21 For then shall be great tribulation, such as was not since the beginning of the world to this time, no, nor ever shall be.

22 And except those days should be shortened, there should no flesh be saved: but for the elect's sake those days shall be shortened.

23 Then if any man shall say unto you, Lo, here is Christ, or there; believe it not.

24 For there shall arise false Christs, and false prophets, and shall shew great signs and wonders; insomuch that, if it were possible, they shall deceive the very elect.

25 Behold, I have told you before.

²⁶ Wherefore if they shall say unto you, Behold, he is in the desert; go not forth: behold, he is in the secret chambers; believe it not.

²⁷ For as the lightning cometh out of the east, and shineth even unto the west; so shall also the coming of the Son of man be.

²⁸ For whosoever the carcase is, there will the eagles be gathered together.

²⁹ Immediately after the tribulation of those days shall the sun be darkened, and the moon shall not give her light, and the stars shall fall from heaven, and the powers of the heavens shall be shaken:

³⁰ And then shall appear the sign of the Son of man in heaven: and then shall all the tribes of the earth mourn, and they shall see the Son of man coming in the clouds of heaven with power and great glory.

³¹ And he shall send his angels with a great sound of a trumpet, and they shall gather together his elect from the four winds, from one end of heaven to the other.

³² Now learn a parable of the fig tree; When his branch is yet tender, and putteth forth leaves, ye know that summer is nigh:

The Scriptures

33 So likewise ye, when ye shall see all these things, know that it is near, even at the doors.

34 Verily I say unto you, this generation shall not pass, till all these things be fulfilled.

35 Heaven and earth shall pass away, but my words shall not pass away.

36 But of that day and hour knoweth no man, no, not the angels of heaven, but my Father only.

37 But as the days of Noe were, so shall also the coming of the Son of man be.

38 For as in the days that were before the flood they were eating and drinking, marrying and giving in marriage, until the day that Noe entered into the ark,

39 And knew not until the flood came, and took them all away; so shall also the coming of the Son of man be.

40 Then shall two be in the field; the one shall be taken, and the other left.

41 Two women shall be grinding at the mill; the one shall be taken, and the other left.

⁴² *Watch therefore: for ye know not what hour your Lord doth come.*

⁴³ *But know this, that if the good man of the house had known in what watch the thief would come, he would have watched, and would not have suffered his house to be broken up.*

⁴⁴ *Therefore be ye also ready: for in such an hour as ye think not the Son of man cometh.*

⁴⁵ *Who then is a faithful and wise servant, whom his lord hath made ruler over his household, to give them meat in due season?*

⁴⁶ *Blessed is that servant, whom his lord when he cometh shall find so doing.*

⁴⁷ *Verily I say unto you, That he shall make him ruler over all his goods.*

⁴⁸ *But and if that evil servant shall say in his heart, My lord delayeth his coming;*

⁴⁹ *And shall begin to smite his fellowservants, and to eat and drink with the drunken;*

⁵⁰ *The lord of that servant shall come in a day when he looketh not for him, and in an hour that he is not aware of,*

The Scriptures

⁵¹ And shall cut him asunder, and appoint him his portion with the hypocrites: there shall be weeping and gnashing of teeth.

"You're right, Dad. I think that I've got a better understanding now. I think I need to read a lot more whenever I can. I think I will read the Book of Revelation. A lot of the guys at church said it's one of the best in trying to explain what's going to happen in the end times."

"Okay boys and you too, young lady. I think it's time to get some rest.

Lord, please keep your Word in the hearts of these boys. I'm sure they will be telling their friends how they spent one day with Jesus this week. Let that knowledge of being with you one day be every day. Amen."

Author's Editorial

As a Christian, one must accept the fact that the Holy Bible is the true Word of God, from the first page to the last page. Have you noticed lately how many people who claim to be Christians do not believe in certain things that the Scriptures speak about? In chapter three I mentioned keeping your eyes on the rulers of this nation. One day they will put you in prison for taking a stand on your beliefs found in God's Word. I was about to submit my work for publication and all of a sudden I held back because I saw on the news a Christian woman being locked up because she refused to go against her beliefs in God's Word. She refused to put her signature on a document which basically says she consents to ungodly behavior according to her beliefs. What about her rights? What about the rights of the gay couple who wanted to get married? Can't we find a solution that both sides could live with?

A simple solution would have been to just change the way the marriage licenses are given. A signature is not really required. Instead, stamp it with a state seal. As long as it has the state, the place, and the names of the recipients, that is all that's really needed. If you need to show proof, is that signature really going to be questioned? I have no signature on my driver's license but it's accepted by any authorized personnel who may need to see it. Can you imagine? 'Sorry sir, you're not allowed to drive with this license because the clerk at the motor vehicle center forgot to sign it.' How stupid are these laws getting today? Again a quick decision was made without any significant thought on the end result. It's a document that gives the spouse marriage benefits. The one performing the act of marriage should be the one with the legal signature approving the legality of marriage. Then, send it back to the state for recording so they can receive marriage benefits. It seems pretty simple to me.

It's not our place to condemn others for the way they live their life. Everyone has the freedom to make that choice for themselves. She did not condemn anyone; she simply took a stand on participating in an ungodly act within her religious beliefs. It was no surprise to me. I saw this coming before it even happened. They say a picture is worth a thousand words. Read a thousand words in God's Word and you may get the picture. Look at all the countries that do not believe in Jesus Christ, should they be blessed by their denial? Do you really believe America will be blessed when we remove '*In God we trust?*' Think again, and keep your eyes open.

Watch what happens to this nation in the next few years. Keep your eyes on the killings today, the weather disasters across our land, the money markets and the actions of your government leadership. God bless America, they say. Sure, as long as you continue to run your nation under the control of the deceiver, I will bless you? At one point I used to be worried about some of these things that I see happening. I got into Gods Word, and I got the picture. It's not a very good-looking picture for this nation.

One day I was talking to a gay gentleman and he said, 'I was born this way, so God must approve.' I said 'Thank you Jesus.' He said, 'Why did you say that?' I said, 'You and a million others were born of that sin and some become adulterers, thieves, liars, and murderers. It's because they were born into sin and have not yet found the Word of God which can change the sinful nature they were born of. You still have a choice. According to God's Word you must be born again. 'What's that?' he says. I said, 'Let me give you some scriptures to read. I think by reading these you will get a better understanding of their meaning. As you're reading Gods Word, open your heart to hear the truth."

That which is born of the flesh is flesh, and that which is born of the Spirit is spirit. (John 3:6)

Jesus answered and said to him, "Truly, truly, I say to you, unless one is born again he cannot see the kingdom of God. (John 3:3)

Blessed be the God and Father of our Lord Jesus Christ, who according to His great mercy has caused us to be born again to a living hope through the resurrection of Jesus Christ from the dead. (1 Peter 1:3)

Then the LORD God formed man of dust from the ground, and breathed into his nostrils the breath of life; and man became a living being. (Genesis 2:7)

Jesus answered and said to him, "Truly, truly, I say to you, unless one is born again he cannot see the kingdom of God." Nicodemus said to Him, "How can a man be born when he is old? He cannot enter a second time into his mother's womb and be born, can he?" Jesus answered, "Truly, truly, I say to you, unless one is born of water and the Spirit he cannot enter into the kingdom of God. (John 3:3-7)

But a natural man does not accept the things of the Spirit of God, for they are foolishness to him; and he cannot understand them, because they are spiritually appraised. (1 Corinthians 2:14)

Since you have in obedience to the truth purified your souls for a sincere love of the brethren, fervently love one another from the heart, for you have been born again not of seed which is perishable but imperishable, that is, through the living and enduring word of God. For, 'all flesh is like grass, and all its glory like the flower of grass. The grass withers, and the flowers fall off. (1 Peter 1:22-25)

I have many friends that are gay or have different religious beliefs. That's not the point. The point is you have a choice to live your life according to your will or according to God's will. My God is a loving God and He has instructed me not to condemn you for your ways, but to love you and share his way of salvation so that you may see the Kingdom of

Author's Editorial

Heaven. We are all born into sin and God clearly says one must be born again in the Spirit to enter the Kingdom of God.

God Bless America and its youth of tomorrow.

Made in the USA
San Bernardino, CA
20 November 2015